1.Edition 2023
ISBN 978-82-693178-5-5 (Paperback)
ISBN 978-82-693178-6-2 (Ebook)
Published by 4DIGITS AS
©2023 4DIGITS

"Give people what they need:
food, medicine, clean air, pure water, trees and grass,
pleasant homes to live in, some hours of work, more
hours of leisure. Don't ask who deserves it. Every
human being deserves it."

Howard Zinn, Marx in Soho

Triathlon Unleashed:

Your Ultimate Guide to Conquer the Swim, Bike, Run

By Alf Erik Malm

Introduction

Inside "Triathlon Unleashed," you'll find a step-by-step approach that takes you from a beginner with big dreams to a confident triathlon warrior. You'll discover how to optimize your swim technique, whether you're a novice in the water or seeking to improve your stroke efficiency. You'll unlock the secrets to cycling like a pro, harnessing speed and power while conquering various terrains. And you'll learn how to unleash your running potential, mastering endurance, pacing, and mental toughness to conquer the final leg of the race.

But this guide goes beyond the physical aspects of triathlon. It delves into the mental game, helping you develop mental resilience, overcome obstacles, and stay focused during training and races. You'll gain valuable insights into race preparation, nutrition, hydration, gear selection, and race-day logistics to ensure you're well-equipped for success.

"Triathlon Unleashed" is not just about finishing a race—it's about embracing a lifestyle of strength, perseverance, and personal growth. It's about challenging yourself, celebrating milestones, and forging lifelong friendships within the vibrant triathlon community.

So, whether you're gearing up for your first sprint triathlon or dreaming of completing an Ironman, "Triathlon Unleashed" will be your comprehensive guidebook, empowering you to conquer the swim, bike, run, and unleash your true triathlon potential.

Are you ready to embark on an incredible journey?

Let's dive in and unlock the true triathlete within you!

The training program focuses on an Olympic distance triathlon, but can be adjusted to other distances.

Triathlon – the beginning:

The sport of triathlon originated in the 1970s and was born out of a friendly competition among athletes from different disciplines. Here's a brief history of how triathlon started:

The exact origins of triathlon are attributed to multiple sources, but the most widely recognized account points to the San Diego Track Club in California. In the mid-1970s, members of the track club began engaging in a multisport event called the "Mission Bay Triathlon," which was organized by Jack Johnstone and Don Shanahan. The event consisted of a run-bike-swim sequence and was held on Mission Bay, San Diego.

However, the first recorded triathlon-like event predates the Mission Bay Triathlon. In 1974, the French sports magazine "L'Équipe" organized an event called "Les Trois Sports" ("The Three Sports") in the town of Meaux, France. This event featured a 10-kilometer run, 800-meter swim, and 67-kilometer bike ride, but it didn't gain widespread attention.

In 1978, the sport of triathlon received significant exposure when the first-ever Hawaiian Iron Man Triathlon took place on the island of Oahu. The event was organized by the couple Judy and John Collins, who combined the existing Waikiki Roughwater Swim, the Around-Oahu Bike Race, and the Honolulu Marathon to create a grueling endurance race.

The Ironman Triathlon became synonymous with the ultimate test of endurance and marked a turning point for the popularity of the sport.

Following the success of the Ironman Triathlon, the sport of triathlon started to gain traction globally. The first International Triathlon Union (ITU) race was held in Avignon, France, in 1989, and the ITU was officially founded the following year. The ITU became the governing body for the sport, overseeing international competitions and establishing standardized rules and regulations.

Since then, triathlon has continued to grow in popularity and has become an Olympic sport. Triathlon made its Olympic debut at the Sydney Games in 2000, featuring a 1.5-kilometer swim, 40-kilometer bike ride, and 10-kilometer run distance for the Olympic distance race.

Today, triathlon is a widely recognized and respected sport, attracting athletes of all levels from around the world. It encompasses various distances, including sprint, Olympic, half Ironman, and full Ironman races, catering to athletes with different goals and abilities.

The sport's growth can be attributed to its unique combination of disciplines, the challenge it presents, and the sense of accomplishment and personal achievement it offers to participants. Triathlon continues to inspire individuals to push their limits, embrace a healthy and active lifestyle, and engage in a supportive and inclusive community.

Who am I?

This year I am turning 50. In my day job, I work to increase the quality of life for people with a disease or who have been in an accident. It is no coincidence that I work in this field. This is what gives my engine full throttle. And of course, sports then, primarily when competing myself, but also by watching others. In the last decade, I have attended many competitions as an athlete. I've participated in several organized activities like running, skiing, and cycling, but mostly triathlons.

I have never been even close to an elite triathlete, but attended my first sprint triathlon 10 years ago.

I've done everything from small short distance local events to Ironmans around the world and Norseman, which is probably the most challenging triathlon in the world. I am also engaged at my local triathlon club and in the Norwegian Triathlon Federation, where I have had the role as Vice-president for 4 years.

What triathlon is

Triathlon is a multi-disciplinary endurance sport that combines swimming, cycling, and running. It is a challenging event that requires athletes to excel in multiple disciplines and transition seamlessly between them. There are various distances in triathlon, each offering its own unique challenges and requirements. In this explanation, we will explore the most common triathlon distances: Sprint, Olympic or Standard, Half Ironman, and Ironman.

1. Sprint Triathlon:
The sprint triathlon is the shortest and most beginner-friendly distance. It is often used as an introduction to the sport and is suitable for athletes of all levels. The standard distances for a sprint triathlon are:

- Swim: The swim portion is typically around 750 meters (0.47 miles). It takes place in a pool or open water, such as a lake or the ocean. The swim can be intimidating for some beginners, but with proper training and technique, it becomes more manageable.

- Bike: The bike leg covers a distance of approximately 20 kilometers (12.4 miles). Athletes ride road bikes or triathlon-specific bikes, depending on their preference and availability. The course is usually on paved roads and may include some rolling hills.

- Run: The run segment in a sprint triathlon is usually around 5 kilometers (3.1 miles). It takes place on roads or trails, and participants can run at a comfortable pace to finish the race.

2. Olympic or Standard Triathlon:

The Olympic or Standard distance triathlon is considered the benchmark distance for the sport. It is a step up from the sprint distance and requires a higher level of fitness and endurance. The standard distances for an Olympic triathlon are:

- Swim: The swim leg covers a distance of approximately 1.5 kilometers (0.93 miles). It takes place in open water, such as a lake or the ocean. Swimmers must be comfortable in deep water and navigate through a marked course.

- Bike: The bike leg in an Olympic triathlon is approximately 40 kilometers (24.8 miles). Athletes ride road bikes or triathlon-specific bikes. The course may include steeper climbs and descents compared to the sprint distance.

- Run: The run segment in an Olympic triathlon is approximately 10 kilometers (6.2 miles). Participants must find their running pace after completing the swim and bike segments, which can be physically demanding.

3. Half Ironman (70.3):

The Half Ironman distance, also known as 70.3, is a significant step up in distance and requires a higher level of training and preparation. The name "70.3" refers to the total mileage covered in the race. The standard distances for a Half Ironman are:

- Swim: The swim leg covers a distance of approximately 1.9 kilometers (1.2 miles). It usually takes place in open water, such as a lake or the ocean. Participants should have strong swimming skills and be prepared for longer periods in the water.

- Bike: The bike leg in a Half Ironman is around 90 kilometers (56 miles). Athletes ride road bikes or triathlon-specific bikes. The course may include challenging terrain and longer climbs, requiring endurance and strength.

- Run: The run segment in a Half Ironman is approximately 21.1 kilometers (13.1 miles), which is a half marathon distance. After completing the swim and bike segments, participants must find the mental and physical stamina to finish the race with a strong run.

4. Ironman (140.6):

The Ironman distance is the pinnacle of triathlon and is renowned for its grueling demands. It is an ultimate test of endurance, pushing athletes to their limits. The name "140.6" represents the total mileage covered in the race. The standard distances for

 an Ironman are:

- Swim: The swim leg covers a distance of approximately 3.8 kilometers (2.4 miles). It takes place in open water, usually in a lake or the ocean. Swimmers must be experienced and confident in their abilities, as well as prepared for longer periods of swimming.

- Bike: The bike leg in an Ironman is around 180 kilometers (112 miles). Athletes ride road bikes or triathlon-specific bikes. The course often includes challenging terrain and demanding climbs, requiring exceptional endurance and strength.

- Run: The run segment in an Ironman is a full marathon distance, approximately 42.2 kilometers (26.2 miles). Participants face the daunting task of running a marathon after completing the swim and bike segments. Mental fortitude and physical stamina are crucial to complete the race.

It's important to note that while these distances represent the standard lengths, there may be variations in specific races. Some events may offer non-standard distances, such as "Sprint Plus" or "Super Sprint," which are slightly longer or shorter than the typical distances. Additionally, the terrain, climate, and course conditions can significantly impact the overall difficulty of the race.

Triathlon distances provide athletes with a range of options, allowing them to challenge themselves at various levels and progress as they gain experience and fitness. Whether you're a beginner or an experienced athlete, triathlon offers a diverse and exciting set of distances to suit different goals and aspirations.

Your first triathlon

For a newbie preparing for their first triathlon, here are some recommendations to ensure a smooth and successful experience:

1. Understand the race requirements: Familiarize yourself with the specific details of the triathlon you'll be participating in. Know the distances, course layout, transition areas, and any specific rules or regulations. This will help you plan and prepare accordingly.

2. Get a medical check-up: Before starting any new physical activity, it's always a good idea to consult with a healthcare professional. They can assess your overall health and provide guidance on any necessary precautions or modifications based on your individual circumstances.

3. Set realistic goals: Determine what you want to achieve in your first triathlon. Set realistic and attainable goals based on your current fitness level and experience. This could be completing the race within a certain time, focusing on enjoying the experience, or simply finishing strong. Having clear goals will help you stay motivated and focused during your training.

4. Start training early: Give yourself ample time to prepare for the triathlon. Develop a training plan that gradually increases in intensity and duration, allowing your body to adapt and avoid overtraining or injuries. Include swimming, cycling, and

running sessions in your training program, as well as transitions between the disciplines to practice the changeovers smoothly.

5. Seek guidance and coaching: If you're new to triathlon, consider working with a coach or joining a triathlon training group. They can provide expert guidance, help you with technique improvements, offer structured training plans, and provide valuable insights into the sport. A coach can also help you with your race strategy and provide tips for the transitions.

6. Practice transitions: Transitions can be a challenging aspect of triathlon. Plan and practice transitioning between each discipline, including the swim-to-bike and bike-to-run transitions. Set up a mock transition area, practice quickly changing gear and attire, and get comfortable with the flow of moving from one discipline to the next. Efficient transitions can save valuable time during the race.

7. Get the right equipment: Invest in essential triathlon gear, such as a well-fitting swimsuit or wetsuit, goggles, a bike suitable for the race distance, a helmet, cycling shoes, and running shoes. Ensure your equipment is comfortable and properly adjusted to prevent discomfort or injury during the race.

8. Practice open water swimming: If your triathlon includes an open water swim, practice swimming in similar conditions to build confidence and improve your technique. Familiarize yourself with sighting (lifting your head to navigate), swimming in a straight line, and dealing with potential challenges like currents or waves.

9. Incorporate brick workouts: Brick workouts involve training two disciplines back-to-back, such as a swim immediately followed by a bike ride or a bike ride followed by a run. This helps your body adapt to the feeling of transitioning between disciplines and improves your overall endurance and conditioning.

10. Focus on nutrition and hydration: Understand the importance of proper nutrition and hydration during training and the race itself. Develop a nutrition plan that suits your body's needs, including pre-race meals, race fueling strategies, and post-race recovery. Practice your nutrition and hydration strategies during training to ensure they work well for you.

11. Rest and recover: Adequate rest and recovery are crucial components of any training plan. Listen to your body and allow for rest days to prevent overtraining and reduce the risk of injuries. Incorporate stretching, foam rolling, and other recovery techniques into your routine to aid in muscle recovery and injury prevention.

12. Participate in a practice race or simulation: Consider participating in a smaller local race or organizing a practice simulation of the triathlon distances. This will give you a taste of the race atmosphere, help you identify any areas for improvement, and build confidence before your main event.

13. Stay positive and enjoy the journey: Triathlon training can be physically and mentally challenging, especially for beginners. Stay positive, celebrate your progress along the way, and remember to enjoy the journey.

Embrace the learning experience, make new friends within the triathlon community, and have fun during the process.

Remember, everyone starts somewhere, and your first triathlon is an exciting milestone. With proper preparation, training, and a positive mindset, you'll be well on your way to crossing that finish line and embracing the accomplishment of completing your first triathlon. Good luck!

Learning to swim 1500 meters

Learning to swim freestyle for 1500 meters requires consistent practice, proper technique, and building endurance. Here are some steps to help you learn and improve your freestyle swimming for longer distances:

1. Get comfortable in the water: If you're new to swimming, start by getting comfortable in the water. Practice floating, submerging your face, and developing basic water confidence. Familiarize yourself with the pool environment and gradually work on your comfort level.

2. Learn the basic freestyle technique: Familiarize yourself with the basic freestyle technique, also known as front crawl. Focus on body position, arm movement, breathing, and kicking. Seek guidance from a swim coach or instructor who can provide proper technique instruction.

3. Practice drills: Incorporate drills into your swimming routine to improve specific aspects of your freestyle technique. Some common drills include:

  - Catch-up drill: Swim with one arm extended while the other arm completes a full stroke. Alternate arms and focus on a complete stroke cycle.

  - Single-arm drill: Swim freestyle using only one arm while keeping the other arm extended in front. Switch arms after a certain distance or time.

   - Kickboard drill: Use a kickboard to focus on your leg kick. Hold the kickboard out in front of you and kick while maintaining a streamlined body position.

   - Breathing drills: Practice bilateral breathing (breathing on both sides) and work on your breathing rhythm and timing.

4. Build endurance gradually: Start with shorter distances and gradually increase the distance you swim over time. Focus on maintaining a steady pace and efficient technique. Incorporate interval training, where you swim shorter distances at a higher intensity, followed by a rest period. This helps build cardiovascular fitness and endurance.

5. Practice open water swimming: If your goal is to swim 1500 meters in open water, practice swimming in open water conditions as much as possible. This will help you become comfortable with factors like currents, waves, and sighting (lifting your head to navigate).

6. Incorporate longer swims: As your endurance improves, gradually increase the distance of your swims. Aim to complete longer continuous swims, gradually building up to the 1500-meter distance. Break the distance into manageable segments and focus on maintaining a consistent pace and technique throughout.

7. Seek guidance and feedback: Consider working with a swim coach or joining a swim group to get guidance, feedback, and technique corrections. Having an experienced coach or swimming community can greatly enhance your learning and progression.

8. Video analysis: Record yourself swimming and review the footage to identify areas for improvement. Compare your technique to that of experienced swimmers or seek feedback from a coach or instructor.

9. Be patient and persistent: Learning to swim freestyle for longer distances takes time and practice. Be patient with yourself and celebrate the progress you make along the way. Consistency and persistence are key to improving your swimming abilities.

Remember to warm up before each swim session, listen to your body, and take rest days to avoid overtraining or injury. Freestyle swimming is a skill that develops with practice and proper technique. With dedication and consistent effort, you can work towards swimming 1500 meters comfortably and efficiently.

Cycling in triathlon

To cycle 40 kilometers fast in a triathlon, it's important to focus on several key aspects: training, technique, equipment, and race strategy. Here are some tips to help you improve your cycling performance in a triathlon:

1. Build cycling-specific fitness: Develop your cycling fitness through regular training rides. Include a mix of endurance rides, interval training, and hill repeats to build strength and aerobic capacity. Gradually increase the distance and intensity of your rides to match the race distance.

2. Work on cycling technique: Proper cycling technique can significantly improve your speed and efficiency. Pay attention to your body position, pedal stroke, and cadence. Maintain a relaxed upper body, engage your core, and focus on smooth and efficient pedal strokes. Consider working with a cycling coach or joining a group ride to get feedback on your technique.

3. Train on race-specific terrain: If possible, incorporate training rides that simulate the course conditions of your triathlon. Practice on similar terrain, including flats, hills, and descents. Familiarize yourself with the route and any challenging sections to develop strategies for pacing and handling different terrain.

4. Optimize your equipment: Ensure your bike is properly fitted to your body and riding style. This includes adjusting saddle height, handlebar position, and cleat alignment. Consider investing in aero bars and aero wheels if allowed in your triathlon. However, it's essential to test and become comfortable with any new equipment before race day.

5. Practice transitions: Transitioning smoothly from the swim to the bike is crucial in a triathlon. Set up a transition area during your training sessions and practice the swim-to-bike transition. Practice mounting your bike quickly and efficiently, putting on your helmet, and getting up to speed smoothly. Efficient transitions can save valuable time during the race.

6. Develop pacing strategies: Determine your target pace for the 40-kilometer distance based on your fitness level and race goals. Pace yourself evenly throughout the ride, avoiding starting too fast and burning out later. Monitor your effort using a heart rate monitor or power meter if available. Familiarize yourself with the course profile and adjust your effort accordingly for climbs, descents, and flats.

7. Learn drafting techniques: Drafting, riding in the slipstream of another cyclist, can significantly improve your speed and conserve energy. Understand the drafting rules of your triathlon and practice riding in a group or with a partner to get comfortable with close proximity riding. Use drafting strategically, but be mindful of safety and the rules of the race.

8. Nutrition and hydration: Proper fueling and hydration are crucial for maintaining energy levels during the bike leg. Develop a nutrition plan and practice it during training rides. Consume a mix of carbohydrates and electrolytes to sustain your energy levels. Stay hydrated by regularly drinking fluids, especially on longer rides.

9. Mental preparation: Mental strength plays a vital role in endurance events. Practice mental techniques such as visualization, positive self-talk, and goal setting to stay focused and motivated during the race. Break the distance into manageable segments and set smaller targets to maintain your mental focus and push through any challenges.

10. Race-day strategy: Plan your race day logistics and strategy in advance. Familiarize yourself with the race course, including any technical sections or potential bottlenecks. Pace yourself according to your training and race goals. Start conservatively and gradually increase your effort as the race progresses. Stay aware of your surroundings, anticipate changes in terrain, and adjust your strategy accordingly.

Remember, improving your cycling performance takes time and consistent training. Be patient, listen to your body, and adjust your training plan as needed. Practice in various conditions and terrains to build your skills and confidence. With focused training, proper technique, and a strategic approach, you can cycle 40 kilometers fast and successfully complete your triathlon.

Running 10K

Here's a sample 6-month training plan to prepare for running a 10-kilometer race. Keep in mind that this plan can be adjusted based on your current fitness level, available time, and individual preferences. It's important to listen to your body, adapt the plan as needed, and consult with a coach or healthcare professional if necessary.

Month 1:
- Week 1-2:
- Start with 3-4 runs per week, focusing on building a running routine.
- Begin with easy-paced runs for 20-30 minutes.
- Gradually increase the duration of each run, adding a few minutes each week.
- Include a cross-training activity such as cycling or swimming on non-running days to build overall fitness and reduce the risk of injury.

- Week 3-4:
- Aim for 4-5 runs per week.
- Include one longer run each week, gradually increasing the distance.
- Add one interval training session per week, incorporating faster-paced intervals followed by recovery periods.
- Continue cross-training activities on non-running days.

Month 2:
- Week 1-2:
- Maintain 4-5 runs per week.
- Increase the distance of your longer run.
- Include hill training sessions to improve strength and endurance.
- Continue with interval training, gradually increasing the intensity and duration of the intervals.

- Week 3-4:
- Aim for 4-5 runs per week.
- Increase the duration of your long run, approaching the target distance of 10 kilometers.
- Incorporate tempo runs at a comfortably challenging pace for building speed and stamina.
- Continue hill training to improve strength and power.

Month 3:
- Week 1-2:
- Maintain 4-5 runs per week.
- Increase the distance of your long run to approximately 8 kilometers.
- Include speed workouts such as fartlek training, alternating between faster and slower segments during your runs.
- Incorporate cross-training activities for active recovery and overall fitness.

- Week 3-4:
- Aim for 4-5 runs per week.
- Increase the duration of your long run, gradually approaching the full 10-kilometer distance.

- Focus on maintaining a steady pace and building mental endurance.
- Continue with speed workouts, alternating between intervals and tempo runs.

Month 4:
- Week 1-2:
- Maintain 4-5 runs per week.
- Include a longer run of approximately 10 kilometers, aiming to complete the target race distance.
- Incorporate interval training sessions with shorter, faster intervals to improve speed and anaerobic fitness.
- Continue with hill training to build strength and power.

- Week 3-4:
- Aim for 4-5 runs per week.
- Continue with the 10-kilometer long run, focusing on maintaining a comfortable pace.
- Include tempo runs at a sustained, moderately challenging pace.
- Incorporate some race-pace runs to get accustomed to running at your target pace.

Month 5:
- Week 1-2:
- Maintain 4-5 runs per week.
- Begin tapering your training volume to allow for recovery and optimal performance.
- Reduce the distance of your long run, but maintain intensity and incorporate some race-pace segments.
- Focus on speed maintenance and mental preparation.

- Week 3-4:
- Further reduce training volume to prioritize rest and recovery.
- Perform shorter, easier runs to stay loose and maintain running fitness.
- Focus on race strategy, visualization, and mental preparation.

Month 6 (Race Week):
- Week 1:
- Rest and recover.

- Perform short, easy runs to keep the body active and maintain a running routine.
  - Stay hydrated and maintain a balanced diet.
  - Focus on mental preparation and visualization of the race.

- Race Day:
  - Follow a proper warm-up routine before the race.
  - Pace yourself according to your training and race strategy.
  - Stay focused, enjoy the experience, and give your best effort.

Remember, it's essential to listen to your body and make adjustments to the plan as needed. If you experience pain or discomfort, consider rest or seeking professional advice. Additionally, prioritize rest, recovery, and proper nutrition to support your training efforts.

6 months training plan for an Olympic distance

Here's a sample 6-month training plan for an Olympic distance triathlon. Keep in mind that this plan can be adjusted based on your current fitness level, available time, and individual preferences. It's always recommended to listen to your body, adapt the plan as needed, and consult with a coach or healthcare professional if necessary.

Month 1:
- Week 1:
  - Swim: 2-3 sessions of 30 minutes each, focusing on technique and building endurance.
  - Bike: 2-3 sessions of 45 minutes each, focusing on building aerobic base.
  - Run: 2-3 sessions of 30 minutes each, focusing on building endurance and establishing a running routine.
  - Incorporate one brick workout (e.g., swim-bike) during the week.

- Week 2-4:
  - Gradually increase the volume and intensity of each discipline. Aim for 3-4 sessions per week for each discipline, gradually increasing duration and distance.
  - Add one interval session for each discipline to work on speed and strength.
  - Continue practicing transitions during brick workouts.

Month 2:
- Week 1-2:
   - Continue with 3-4 sessions per week for each discipline.
   - Focus on building endurance and improving technique.
   - Incorporate longer bike rides, gradually increasing distance.
   - Increase the duration of the long run to build running endurance.
   - Practice brick workouts with longer distances.

- Week 3-4:
   - Continue with 3-4 sessions per week for each discipline.
   - Introduce hill training for cycling and running.
   - Incorporate open water swimming practice if applicable.
   - Add one tempo or speed session for each discipline to improve overall speed and fitness.

Month 3:
- Week 1-2:
   - Continue with 3-4 sessions per week for each discipline.
   - Increase the distance and intensity of the long bike ride.
   - Increase the distance of the long run, gradually approaching the Olympic distance.
   - Incorporate transition practices within brick workouts.

- Week 3-4:
   - Continue with 3-4 sessions per week for each discipline.
   - Focus on building endurance and maintaining speed.
   - Incorporate race-specific simulations, including swim-to-bike and bike-to-run transitions.
   - Practice pacing strategies for each discipline.

Month 4:
- Week 1-2:
    - Maintain 3-4 sessions per week for each discipline.
    - Continue with long rides and runs, gradually increasing distance.
    - Incorporate speed and interval sessions to improve race pace.

- Week 3-4:
    - Start tapering the training volume to allow for recovery and optimal performance.
    - Reduce overall training load while maintaining intensity.
    - Focus on fine-tuning technique and mental preparation.

Month 5:
- Week 1-2:
    - Continue tapering, reducing training volume further.
    - Maintain shorter, higher-intensity sessions to maintain race readiness.
    - Focus on mental preparation, visualization, and race strategy.

- Week 3-4:
    - Further reduce training volume.
    - Focus on recovery, stretching, and relaxation techniques.
    - Review race logistics and prepare necessary equipment.

Month 6 (Race Week):
- Week 1:
    - Rest and recover.
    - Perform short, easy workouts to keep the body active.
    - Stay hydrated and maintain a balanced diet.
    - Focus on mental preparation and visualization of the race.

- Race Day:
    - Follow a proper warm-up routine before each discipline.
    - Pace yourself according to your training and race strategy.
    - Stay focused, enjoy the experience, and give your best
effort.

Remember to listen to your body throughout the training
plan. If you experience any pain or discomfort, consider rest or
seeking professional advice. Additionally, don't forget to
prioritize rest, recovery, and proper nutrition to support your
training efforts. Good luck with your Olympic distance
triathlon!

Nutrition and Hydration

Securing proper nutrition and hydration during an Olympic distance triathlon is crucial to maintain your energy levels and performance throughout the race. Here are some tips to help you plan and execute your nutrition and hydration strategy:

1. Pre-race nutrition: Focus on consuming a balanced meal rich in carbohydrates the night before the race. This will help top up your glycogen stores. On the morning of the race, have a light, easily digestible meal that includes carbohydrates and some protein. Experiment during your training to find out what works best for your body.

2. Hydration before the race: Start hydrating well before the race begins. Drink water or a sports drink to ensure you're properly hydrated. Avoid excessive caffeine and alcohol consumption, as they can dehydrate you.

3. Plan your race nutrition: Calculate your estimated race duration and plan your nutrition and hydration strategy accordingly. Aim to consume 30-60 grams of carbohydrates per hour during the race to maintain your energy levels. This can come from sports drinks, energy gels, energy bars, or real food options like bananas or energy chews.

4. Use sports drinks: Sports drinks provide a combination of carbohydrates and electrolytes, which are crucial for maintaining hydration and replacing electrolyte losses.

Choose a sports drink that you have tested and tolerated well during your training, and carry it in a hydration system or bottles mounted on your bike.

5. Energy gels and bars: Energy gels and bars are convenient options for quick and easily digestible energy during the race. They provide a concentrated source of carbohydrates that can be consumed on the bike or during the run. Experiment with different brands and flavors during your training to find what works best for you.

6. Hydration during the race: Carry water bottles on your bike to stay hydrated throughout the cycling leg. Take regular sips of water to prevent dehydration. If you're prone to cramping, consider adding an electrolyte tablet or powder to your water to replenish electrolytes lost through sweating.

7. Break your nutrition and hydration into segments: Divide your race into segments (e.g., swim, bike, run) and plan when and how much nutrition and hydration you'll consume during each leg. Set reminders or use the mile markers as cues to take in fluids and fuel. Practice this strategy during your training to establish a routine.

8. Aid stations: Take advantage of aid stations during the race. Know their locations beforehand and plan accordingly. Grab water or sports drinks as needed, and use the opportunity to refill your water bottles or grab additional nutrition if necessary.

9. Listen to your body: Everyone's nutritional needs are different, so pay attention to your body's signals. Drink when you're thirsty, and consume fuel as needed. Avoid waiting until you feel extremely hungry or thirsty before taking in nutrition or hydration.

10. Practice during training: Use your training sessions to practice your nutrition and hydration strategy. Experiment with different products, timings, and quantities to determine what works best for you. This will help you fine-tune your plan and ensure you're comfortable with your chosen fueling options.

Remember, it's important to test your nutrition and hydration strategy during your training sessions to identify what works best for you. Every individual is unique, so use your training period to experiment and find the right combination of products and timings that optimize your performance and keep you comfortable throughout the race.

Transition

Efficiently transitioning from swimming to cycling in a triathlon can save you valuable time during the race. Here are some tips to help you make a fast and smooth transition:

1. Mental preparation: Visualize and mentally rehearse your transition before the race. Familiarize yourself with the transition area layout, entry and exit points, and the location of your bike. Mentally walk through the steps of your transition, visualizing yourself moving swiftly and confidently.

2. Layout and organize your transition area: Set up your transition area in a clean and organized manner to minimize confusion and maximize efficiency. Lay out your cycling gear and equipment in a logical order, such as placing your helmet, sunglasses, socks, and cycling shoes in a sequence that makes sense to you.

3. Practice your transition during training: Incorporate transition practice into your training sessions to refine your process. Simulate the swim-to-bike transition by exiting the water and quickly moving to your transition area. Practice removing your wetsuit or swim gear efficiently and smoothly. Put on your helmet and cycling shoes swiftly, and mount your bike as quickly as possible.

4. Use a transition mat: Place a brightly colored transition mat or towel next to your bike to mark your spot and make it

easier to locate. This visual cue can help you find your area quickly and avoid wasting time searching for your gear.

5. Leave your shoes clipped to your bike: If you're comfortable with it, leave your cycling shoes clipped into your pedals. This allows you to run barefoot or in socks from the swim to your bike, saving time on putting on your shoes. Once you're on your bike, slip your feet into the shoes and secure them.

6. Pre-open and position your shoes: If you prefer not to leave your shoes clipped to your bike, pre-open the straps or fasteners on your cycling shoes and position them ready for you to slip your feet in quickly. This eliminates the need to fumble with tightening the straps or fasteners during the transition.

7. Use elastic laces: Consider replacing regular shoelaces with elastic laces in your running shoes. Elastic laces allow for quick and easy slip-on/off without the need for tying knots. This can save valuable time during the transition.

8. Practice mounting and dismounting your bike: Work on your bike-mounting and bike-dismounting technique to ensure a smooth and efficient transition onto and off your bike. Practice mounting your bike by running alongside it and jumping onto the saddle while maintaining forward momentum. Similarly, practice dismounting by smoothly swinging your leg over the back of the bike while approaching the dismount line.

9. Minimize distractions: Stay focused and avoid distractions during the transition. Maintain a clear mental checklist of the necessary steps and avoid engaging in conversations or

getting caught up in the energy of the transition area. Stay in the zone and remain focused on the task at hand.

10. Stay calm and composed: Keep your composure during the transition, even if things don't go exactly as planned. If you encounter a small setback or make a mistake, take a deep breath, quickly adjust, and continue with the transition. Staying calm and composed will help you maintain efficiency and prevent unnecessary time loss.

Remember, practicing your transition and familiarizing yourself with the process can significantly improve your speed and efficiency. By optimizing your setup, streamlining your movements, and staying focused, you can make the swim-to-bike transition as fast and smooth as possible in a triathlon.

Be prepared - Mentally

Mental preparation is crucial for a successful first Olympic distance triathlon. Here are some tips to help you mentally prepare for the race:

1. Set realistic goals: Define your goals for the race based on your current fitness level, training, and experience. Set both outcome goals (such as finishing within a certain time) and process goals (such as maintaining good form throughout the race). Ensure your goals are challenging yet attainable, and focus on personal improvement rather than comparing yourself to others.

2. Visualize success: Use visualization techniques to mentally rehearse the race. Close your eyes and imagine yourself going through each leg of the triathlon confidently and successfully. Visualize overcoming challenges, staying calm, and crossing the finish line with a sense of accomplishment. The more vividly you can imagine it, the more it can translate into reality.

3. Positive self-talk: Cultivate a positive mindset by using positive self-talk. Replace any negative or self-doubting thoughts with positive affirmations. Remind yourself of your training efforts, strengths, and capabilities. Use phrases like "I am prepared," "I am strong," and "I can do this" to boost your confidence and motivation.

4. Focus on the process: Rather than getting overwhelmed by the entire race distance, focus on the present moment and the task at hand. Break down the race into smaller segments, such as the swim, transition, bike, and run. Concentrate on executing each segment to the best of your ability without getting ahead of yourself.

5. Practice relaxation techniques: Learn and practice relaxation techniques, such as deep breathing, progressive muscle relaxation, or meditation. These techniques can help calm your mind, reduce anxiety, and keep you focused and centered during the race. Incorporate them into your training routine to familiarize yourself with their benefits.

6. Create a race-day plan: Develop a detailed race-day plan that covers logistics, nutrition, hydration, transitions, and pacing. Having a well-thought-out plan will help alleviate stress and provide a sense of control. Review your plan several times, visualize yourself executing it smoothly, and make any necessary adjustments based on the race conditions.

7. Embrace the unknown: Accept that unexpected situations can arise during the race, and mentally prepare yourself to adapt and problem-solve. Anticipate potential challenges, such as race-day weather conditions or equipment malfunctions, and have contingency plans in mind. Being mentally flexible and adaptable will help you navigate any surprises that come your way.

8. Seek support: Surround yourself with a supportive network of family, friends, or fellow triathletes who can provide encouragement and motivation. Share your goals and concerns with them, and lean on their support during your training and on race day. Consider joining a local triathlon club or online community to connect with like-minded individuals who understand the challenges and triumphs of triathlon.

9. Reflect on your training: Take confidence in the training you've completed leading up to the race. Reflect on the progress you've made, the obstacles you've overcome, and the hard work you've put in. Trust in your training and believe in your ability to perform on race day.

10. Enjoy the experience: Finally, remember to have fun and enjoy the experience. Triathlons are about challenging yourself, testing your limits, and celebrating your achievements. Embrace the excitement, the camaraderie, and the sense of accomplishment that comes with crossing the finish line of your first Olympic distance triathlon.

By incorporating these mental preparation techniques into your training and race-day routine, you'll be better equipped to handle any challenges that arise and perform at your best during your first Olympic distance triathlon.

Join a club

Joining a triathlon club can offer numerous benefits and advantages for triathletes at all levels of experience and ability. Here are several reasons why you should consider joining a triathlon club:

1. Training Support and Structure: Triathlon clubs provide a structured and supportive environment for training. You'll have access to organized group workouts led by experienced coaches or seasoned athletes who can guide you in improving your technique, endurance, and performance in swimming, cycling, and running. Club training sessions often include specific workouts, intervals, and drills tailored to triathlon preparation.

2. Motivation and Accountability: Training alongside fellow club members can provide an extra dose of motivation and accountability. Being part of a community that shares similar goals and passions can help you stay committed to your training plan, push through challenging workouts, and celebrate achievements together. The camaraderie and friendly competition within the club can boost your motivation and make training more enjoyable.

3. Knowledge and Experience Sharing: Triathlon clubs bring together athletes with various levels of experience and expertise. By joining a club, you gain access to a wealth of knowledge and experience from seasoned triathletes.

You can tap into their insights, learn from their successes and failures, and benefit from their guidance on training techniques, race strategies, equipment, and nutrition. This shared wisdom can accelerate your progress as a triathlete.

4. Networking and Social Connections: Triathlon clubs offer opportunities to expand your network and make social connections with like-minded individuals. You'll meet people who share your passion for the sport and can relate to the challenges and triumphs of triathlon training and racing. Building relationships within the triathlon community can lead to lifelong friendships, training partnerships, and a support system that extends beyond the training sessions.

5. Access to Resources and Discounts: Many triathlon clubs have partnerships with local businesses, sponsors, and event organizers. As a club member, you may enjoy benefits such as discounted race entries, exclusive access to training facilities, gear discounts, and special deals on coaching services and sports nutrition products. These perks can help you save money and enhance your overall triathlon experience.

6. Group Training and Racing Opportunities: Triathlon clubs often organize group training sessions, including swim, bike, and run workouts. These sessions can provide a structured and supportive environment to push your limits, practice race-specific skills, and simulate race scenarios. Additionally, clubs may organize or participate in team relay events or triathlon races, offering opportunities to compete together as a team and share the excitement of race day.

7. Mentorship and Guidance: Triathlon clubs often have experienced athletes who are willing to serve as mentors or

coaches for newer members. Having a mentor can provide personalized guidance, advice, and feedback on your training, race preparation, and overall development as a triathlete. They can help you set realistic goals, navigate challenges, and optimize your training plan based on their own experiences.

8. Triathlon Club Events and Social Activities: Triathlon clubs frequently organize social events, workshops, educational seminars, and guest speaker sessions that cover various aspects of the sport. These events create opportunities to expand your knowledge, learn from experts, and connect with other triathletes outside of training. They also foster a sense of community and fun beyond the physical aspects of triathlon.

Joining a triathlon club can enhance your triathlon journey by providing a supportive community, valuable resources, expert guidance, and an enjoyable social experience. It can take your training, performance, and overall triathlon experience to the next level while fostering a love for the sport and a lifelong passion for triathlon.

Getting a coach?

If you are looking to hire a triathlon coach, there are several important factors to consider to ensure you find the right coach for your needs. Here are some key aspects to look for:

1. Qualifications and experience: Check the coach's qualifications, certifications, and experience in coaching triathletes. Look for coaches who have relevant certifications from recognized organizations, such as USA Triathlon or the International Triathlon Coaching Association. Additionally, consider their experience working with athletes at your level and with similar goals.

2. Coaching philosophy and approach: Understand the coach's coaching philosophy and approach. Determine if their coaching style aligns with your own preferences and needs. Some coaches may emphasize structured training plans, while others focus more on individualized coaching or technique development. It's important to find a coach who resonates with your goals, personality, and preferred training methods.

3. Communication and accessibility: Communication is key in a coaching relationship. Ensure that the coach is accessible and responsive to your questions, concerns, and progress updates.
Find out how frequently you can expect to communicate with your coach and the methods of communication they

prefer (e.g., email, phone calls, in-person meetings). Open and clear
communication will help you receive timely guidance and feedback.

4. Personalized training plans: Look for a coach who can provide personalized training plans tailored to your specific goals, abilities, and schedule. A customized plan takes into account your strengths, weaknesses, and any limitations you may have. This individualized approach will help you optimize your training and progress effectively.

5. Track record and testimonials: Research the coach's track record and reputation. Look for testimonials or reviews from other athletes they have coached. Positive feedback and success stories from athletes can indicate the coach's ability to help athletes reach their goals and perform at their best. Don't hesitate to ask the coach for references or contact previous clients for their insights.

6. Compatibility and rapport: A good coach-athlete relationship is built on trust, respect, and open communication. Consider whether you feel comfortable working with the coach and if you believe they understand your needs and goals. A positive rapport with your coach will contribute to a productive and enjoyable coaching experience.

7. Support services: Inquire about any additional support services the coach offers, such as strength training guidance, nutrition advice, or race strategy planning. These supplementary services can provide valuable support and expertise in areas beyond the training plan.

8. Cost and commitment: Understand the coach's pricing structure and payment terms. Determine if the cost aligns with your budget and if the coach offers different coaching packages to suit different needs. Additionally, clarify the commitment required, including the duration of the coaching relationship and any cancellation policies.

9. Continuous education and professional development: A coach committed to their own professional development and staying up-to-date with the latest training techniques and research is a valuable asset. Inquire about their ongoing education efforts, attendance at coaching conferences, or involvement in coaching communities. A coach who continually seeks to improve their knowledge and skills can offer you the most effective guidance.

10. Trial period or consultation: Many coaches offer a trial period or initial consultation to assess compatibility and determine if they can meet your needs. Take advantage of this opportunity to have a conversation with the coach, ask questions, and gauge their expertise and suitability for your goals.

Finding the right triathlon coach is a personal decision, and it's important to take the time to research, interview, and consider your options. Trust your instincts and choose a coach who inspires confidence, understands your goals, and can provide the guidance and support you need to succeed in your triathlon journey.

Common mistakes first timers do

First-time triathletes often make a few common mistakes as they navigate the challenges of training and competing in their first triathlon. Being aware of these mistakes can help you avoid them and have a more successful experience. Here are some of the most common mistakes:

1. Inadequate or unbalanced training: One of the most common mistakes is not dedicating enough time to training or neglecting specific disciplines. It's important to follow a structured training plan that includes a balance of swim, bike, and run workouts, as well as strength and flexibility training. Neglecting any of the disciplines can lead to imbalances and affect overall performance.

2. Neglecting brick workouts: Brick workouts involve training two disciplines back-to-back, such as biking immediately followed by running. Many first-time triathletes underestimate the impact of transitioning between disciplines and don't practice brick workouts enough. Incorporating regular brick sessions into your training can help your body adapt to the specific demands of the triathlon.

3. Not practicing open water swimming: Pool swimming is different from swimming in open water, which can be more challenging due to factors like waves, currents, and limited visibility. Failing to practice open water swimming before the race can lead to anxiety and poor performance. It's crucial to

get comfortable swimming in open water and practice sighting techniques and navigating in different conditions.

4. Ignoring race day logistics and transitions: Transitions play a significant role in triathlon, and first-time triathletes often overlook the importance of transition area setup, knowing the layout, and practicing transitions. Familiarize yourself with the race venue, understand the flow of the transition area, and practice transitioning between disciplines during training to improve efficiency and save time on race day.

5. Not pacing properly: Pacing is crucial in a triathlon, especially for longer distances. Many first-time triathletes get caught up in the excitement of the race and start too fast, leading to fatigue and decreased performance later on. It's important to have a race strategy and stick to a sustainable pace that allows you to finish strong in all three disciplines.

6. Poor nutrition and hydration planning: Nutrition and hydration are often overlooked by first-time triathletes. Failing to fuel properly before, during, and after the race can lead to fatigue, cramping, and decreased performance. Practice your nutrition and hydration strategy during training to find what works best for you and ensure you have a plan for race day.

7. Not practicing race-day scenarios: First-time triathletes may not have experience with the specific challenges and logistics of a triathlon race. It's important to practice race-day scenarios during training, such as simulating race distances, practicing transitions, and testing equipment and gear.

This helps you become familiar with the demands of the race and ensures you're prepared for any unforeseen circumstances.

8. Overtraining or inadequate recovery: Some first-time triathletes may push themselves too hard during training, leading to overtraining and increased risk of injury or burnout. On the other hand, some may not give themselves enough time to recover and adapt to the training load. Finding the right balance between training intensity and adequate recovery is crucial for progress and injury prevention.

9. Neglecting mental preparation: Triathlon is not only physically demanding but also mentally challenging. First-time triathletes may overlook mental preparation, such as managing race-day nerves, staying focused during the race, and maintaining a positive mindset. Incorporating mental training techniques, such as visualization and positive self-talk, can help enhance performance and enjoyment.

10. Comparing yourself to others: It's common for first-time triathletes to compare themselves to more experienced athletes or have unrealistic expectations. Remember that everyone has a unique journey, and focus on your own progress and enjoyment. Celebrate your accomplishments and use the experience as an opportunity to learn and grow as a triathlete.

By being aware of these common mistakes, you can take proactive steps to avoid them and have a more successful and enjoyable first triathlon experience.

Triathlon has a number of iconic races that are renowned for their challenging courses, rich history, and professional athlete participation. Here are some of the most iconic triathlon races around the world:

The most iconic races in triathlon:

Ironman World Championship (Kona, Hawaii): The Ironman World Championship held in Kona, Hawaii is perhaps the most famous and prestigious triathlon race. It takes place annually in October and features a 2.4-mile (3.86 km) swim, a 112-mile (180.25 km) bike ride, and a 26.2-mile (42.2 km) marathon run. Known for its grueling conditions and iconic lava fields, this race attracts top professional athletes and age-group triathletes who qualify through other Ironman events.

Escape from Alcatraz Triathlon (San Francisco, USA): The Escape from Alcatraz Triathlon is an iconic race held in San Francisco, California. It starts with a 1.5-mile (2.4 km) swim from Alcatraz Island to the mainland, followed by an 18-mile (29 km) bike ride and an 8-mile (13 km) run through the challenging hills and trails of the city. The unique swim course, with its chilly water and strong currents, adds to the race's mystique.

Challenge Roth (Roth, Germany): Challenge Roth is one of the world's largest and most popular long-distance triathlons. Held in Roth, Germany, it features a 2.4-mile (3.86 km) swim in the Main-Danube Canal, a 112-mile (180.25 km) bike ride through the scenic Franconian countryside, and a marathon run. Known for its enthusiastic crowd support, festive atmosphere, and fast course, it has become a bucket list race for many triathletes.

Norseman Xtreme Triathlon (Eidfjord, Norway): The Norseman Xtreme Triathlon is renowned for its extreme and rugged nature. It starts with a chilly 2.4-mile (3.86 km) swim in a fjord, followed by a demanding 112-mile (180.25 km) bike ride through steep mountain passes, and finishes with a marathon run that includes a grueling ascent up Gaustatoppen, the highest mountain in Norway. This race attracts athletes seeking a true test of endurance and adventure.

London Triathlon (London, UK): The London Triathlon is one of the largest and most iconic triathlon events in the world. Held in the heart of London, it features various race distances, including super-sprint, sprint, and Olympic distances. The event attracts a diverse range of participants, from elite athletes to first-time triathletes, and provides a unique experience of racing through the city's iconic landmarks.

ITU World Triathlon Series Grand Final (Various Locations): The ITU World Triathlon Series Grand Final is the pinnacle event of the ITU World Triathlon Series. It brings together elite and age-group triathletes from around the world to compete for the overall series championship. The race locations vary each year, showcasing stunning courses in iconic cities, such as Gold Coast, Yokohama, and Edmonton.

These races represent just a few of the many iconic triathlon events around the world. Each race offers its own unique challenges, experiences, and atmosphere, making them highly sought after by triathletes of all levels. Participating in one of these iconic races can provide an unforgettable triathlon experience and create lasting memories.

The next level – becoming better

Becoming a good triathlete requires a combination of factors and a commitment to consistent training and improvement. While there is no single secret to success, here are some key elements that contribute to becoming a good triathlete:

1. Goal Setting: Set clear and realistic goals that align with your abilities and aspirations. Goals provide direction and motivation, helping you stay focused and committed throughout your triathlon journey. Break down your goals into short-term and long-term objectives to track progress and celebrate milestones along the way.

2. Consistent Training: Triathlon is a demanding sport that requires training in three disciplines—swimming, cycling, and running. Consistency is key to building endurance, improving technique, and developing strength in each discipline. Create a training plan that balances all three sports and includes structured workouts tailored to your abilities and goals.

3. Cross-Training and Strength Training: Incorporate cross-training activities and strength training into your routine. Cross-training helps prevent overuse injuries and improves overall fitness by engaging different muscle groups. Strength training enhances power, stability, and injury prevention. Focus on exercises that target the specific muscle groups used in swimming, cycling, and running.

4. Proper Technique: Invest time in learning and refining proper technique for each discipline. Efficient technique improves performance and reduces the risk of injury. Consider working with a coach or attending clinics to receive guidance and feedback on your form. Practice drills and exercises that specifically target technique improvement in swimming, cycling, and running.

5. Nutrition and Hydration: Pay attention to your nutrition and hydration to support optimal performance and recovery. Fuel your body with a well-balanced diet that provides the necessary macronutrients (carbohydrates, protein, and fats) and micronutrients (vitamins and minerals). Develop a nutrition and hydration plan for training and racing to ensure you maintain energy levels and stay properly hydrated.

6. Mental Preparation: Triathlon requires mental fortitude and resilience. Develop mental strategies to manage pre-race nerves, stay focused during training and racing, and overcome challenges. Techniques such as visualization, positive self-talk, and mindfulness can help enhance mental strength and performance.

7. Rest and Recovery: Adequate rest and recovery are essential for progress and injury prevention. Listen to your body and prioritize rest days, active recovery sessions, and sufficient sleep. Incorporate stretching, foam rolling, and other recovery modalities into your routine to promote muscle repair and reduce the risk of overuse injuries.

8. Race Experience: Gain race experience by participating in smaller local races before tackling larger and more challenging events. Race experience allows you to practice

transitions, pacing, and race-day logistics. Learn from each race to identify areas for improvement and build confidence for future events.

9. Support Network: Surround yourself with a supportive network of fellow triathletes, training partners, and coaches. Training with others can provide motivation, accountability, and valuable insights. Seek guidance and advice from experienced triathletes and coaches who can offer expertise and support throughout your triathlon journey.

10. Enjoyment and Balance: Lastly, remember to enjoy the process and maintain balance in your life. Triathlon is a demanding sport, but it should also bring joy and fulfillment. Find ways to make training enjoyable, celebrate achievements, and strike a balance between training, work, personal life, and rest.

Becoming a good triathlete is a journey that requires patience, dedication, and a growth mindset. Embrace the process, stay committed to your goals, and continuously seek opportunities for improvement.

12 stars of triathlon

Here are 12 famous triathletes who have made significant contributions to the sport:

1. Chrissie Wellington (Great Britain)
2. Jan Frodeno (Germany)
3. Simon Whitfield (Canada)
4. Gwen Jorgensen (United States)
5. Javier Gómez Noya (Spain)
6. Emma Snowsill (Australia)
7. Alistair Brownlee (Great Britain)
8. Mirinda Carfrae (Australia)
9. Flora Duffy (Bermuda)
10. Craig Alexander (Australia)
11. Kristian Blummenfelt (Norway)
12. Gustav Iden (Norway)

1. **Chrissie Wellington** (Great Britain): Chrissie Wellington is a four-time Ironman World Champion (2007, 2008, 2009, 2011) and is considered one of the greatest female triathletes of all time. She retired from professional racing in 2012 but left a lasting impact on the sport with her dominance and numerous course records.

2. **Jan Frodeno** (Germany): Jan Frodeno is a German triathlete who won the gold medal at the 2008 Beijing Olympics. He then transitioned to long-distance racing and became a three-time Ironman World Champion (2015, 2016, 2019).

Frodeno is known for his exceptional talent and consistently strong performances.

3. **Simon Whitfield** (Canada): Simon Whitfield is a Canadian triathlete who won the gold medal at the inaugural Olympic triathlon in Sydney in 2000. He also competed in four subsequent Olympic Games and had a successful career in ITU racing, earning multiple World Championship podium finishes.

4. **Gwen Jorgensen** (United States): Gwen Jorgensen is an American triathlete who won the gold medal at the 2016 Rio Olympics, becoming the first American woman to achieve this feat. She dominated the ITU circuit for several years and transitioned to long-distance racing after the Olympics.

5. **Javier Gómez Noya** (Spain): Javier Gómez Noya is a Spanish triathlete and one of the most accomplished athletes in the sport. He has won multiple ITU World Championships, including the 2012 ITU World Triathlon Series, and has consistently been among the top contenders in both short and long-distance races.

6. **Emma Snowsill** (Australia): Emma Snowsill is an Australian triathlete who won the gold medal at the 2008 Beijing Olympics. She was a dominant force in ITU racing during her career, with multiple World Championship titles and a reputation for her strong swim and bike performances.

7. **Alistair Brownlee** (Great Britain): Alistair Brownlee is a British triathlete who won the gold medal at the 2012 and 2016 Olympics. He has also achieved success in ITU racing,

with multiple World Championship titles and a reputation for his exceptional running ability.

8. **Mirinda Carfrae** (Australia): Mirinda Carfrae, also known as "Rinny," is an Australian triathlete who has had tremendous success in long-distance racing. She is a three-time Ironman World Champion (2010, 2013, 2014) and has set multiple course records. Carfrae is particularly known for her strong running ability.

9. **Flora Duffy** (Bermuda): Flora Duffy is a triathlete from Bermuda who won the gold medal at the 2018 Commonwealth Games and the gold medal at the 2021 Tokyo Olympics. She has been a dominant force in ITU racing, with multiple World Championship titles and a strong all-around performance.

10. **Craig Alexander** (Australia): Craig Alexander, also known as "Crowie," is an Australian triathlete and one of the most successful long-distance triathletes. He is a three-time Ironman World Champion (2008, 2009, 2011) and has set numerous course records. Alexander is admired for his consistency and longevity in the sport.

11. **Kristian Blummenfelt** is a Norwegian triathlete who has made significant contributions to the sport. He achieved notable success in ITU racing and has transitioned to long-distance racing as well. Blummenfelt won the gold medal at the 2020 Tokyo Olympics, delivering a remarkable performance that showcased his strength and determination. He has also achieved success on the ITU World Triathlon Series circuit, earning podium finishes and demonstrating his versatility as a triathlete. Blummenfelt's talent and

accomplishments have earned him a place among the elite triathletes in the world.

12. **Gustav Iden**, also from Norway, has made a name for himself in the world of triathlon. He achieved a breakthrough victory at the 2019 Ironman 70.3 World Championship, where he defeated some of the sport's top athletes. Iden showcased his potential and talent with a strong performance across the swim, bike, and run disciplines. His victory propelled him into the spotlight and established him as a force to be reckoned with in the triathlon world. Gustav Iden's accomplishments make him a notable triathlete in his own right.

These triathletes have achieved remarkable success in the sport of triathlon and have left a lasting impact on the triathlon community through their performances, records, and dedication to the sport.

Norseman Triathlon

Norseman Xtreme Triathlon is rated as the most challenging triathlon in the world. Their slogan, "This is not for you," sends many people away before trying. However, contrary to what we naturally expect, more people are interested in trying it out. Perhaps, they are all curious or big on sports like I am. Hence, even though the race is hard, getting a start number is harder. Every year 5000 people attend a lottery to get one of the 250 start slots.

By 2021 had tried for six years to get a spot but did not get one. Then the pandemic gave me an opening since some of the athletes could not travel abroad. 6 weeks before the race, I got an email with an invitation to join in and grabbed it without hesitating. Norseman is something special and every triathlete's dream.

The race starts with a 3.8-kilometer swim in a fjord in Norway at 05.00 AM. We were transported by a ferry in the dark, and the sea got heavier and heavier the more we moved from the starting point. Usually, I would use 1 hour and 15 minutes swimming this distance, but this morning, I spent over 2 hours in cold water with challenging waves and currents. On the way to my bike, I felt like I had swallowed a fjord of salt water and was tired and dizzy.

On the bike leg, you start with a 1000-meter climb up a mountain plateau. Entering the plateau, I met a headwind of 20 m/s and some rain. My schedule was already history, and now it was all about finishing. After almost 9 hours on the bike, I had done 180 kilometers and climbed 2800 meters on the bike. I was exhausted and had nothing to eat since the swim. I was cold and wet, but the motivation was still there.

The finish line is on top of a mountain called Gaustadtoppen. It is 1800 meters above sea level, so the climbing was not over. I picked up another athlete sitting freezing in the transition zone, and we decided to finish this together. The rain was constant, but we kept the mood up by sharing our misery. Sometimes one plus one is more than two, and this was one of those moments. At midnight in the dark, we passed the finish line together. The two last ones to finish the race that year, 19 hours after the start. Although all my ambitions for a good result were crushed, I was still proud. Proud to have finished, and to have put myself in a position to undertake such a challenge at the age of 47.

To me triathlon is about achieving my goals together with people with the same interest. But it`s also about keeping a good health.

Good luck on your first triathlon.

Alf Erik Malm